HOLIDAYS AND FESTIVALS

Veterans Day

Rebecca Rissman

Heinemann Library
Chicago, Illinois

www.heinemannraintree.com
Visit our website to find out more information about Heinemann-Raintree books.

To order:

☎ Phone 888-454-2279

💻 Visit www.heinemannraintree.com to browse our catalog and order online.

Edited by Adrian Vigliano and Rebecca Rissman
Designed by Ryan Frieson
Picture research by Tracy Cummins
Leveling by Nancy E. Harris
Originated by Capstone Global Library Ltd.
Printed in China by South China Printing Company Ltd.

15 14 13 12 11 10
10 9 8 7 6 5 4 3 2 1

Library of Congress Cataloging-in-Publication Data
Rissman, Rebecca.
  Veterans Day / Rebecca Rissman.
    p. cm.—(Holidays and festivals)
  Includes bibliographical references and index.
  ISBN 978-1-4329-4053-9 (hc)—ISBN 978-1-4329-4072-0 (pbk.) 1.
Veterans Day—Juvenile literature. I. Title.
  D671.R57 2010
  394.264—dc22
                                       2009052852

Acknowledgments

The author and publishers are grateful to the following for permission to reproduce copyright material: Corbis ©Michael Reynolds/epa **p.6**; Corbis ©MICHAEL REYNOLDS/epa **p.9**; Corbis © Bettmann **p.11**; Corbis ©SHAMIL ZHUMATOV/Reuters **p.13**; Corbis ©JEFF ZELEVANSKY/Reuters **p.15**; Corbis ©Kevin Dodge **p.16**; Corbis ©Jeffrey Markowitz/Sygma **p.17**; Corbis ©Gabe Palmer **p.20**; Corbis ©MICHAEL REYNOLDS/epa **p.23a**; Corbis ©Bettmann **p.23b**; DefenseImagery.mil **p.8**; Department of Defense/Cherie Cullen **p.18**; Department of Defense/Cherie Cullen **p.23c**; Getty Images/Jason Dewey **p.4**; Getty Images/Chip Somodevilla **p.19**; istockphoto ©Leo Blanchette **p.22**; U.S. Navy photo/MC2 Mark Logico **p.5**; U.S. Navy photo/MCSN Sheldon Rowley **p.7**; U.S. Air Force photo/SrA Jason Epley **p.10**; U.S. Air Force photo/Tech. Sgt. Dawn M. Anderson **p.12**; U.S. Navy photo/MC2 Maebel Tinoko **p.14**; U.S. Navy photo/MC2 Joshua J. Wah **p.21**.

Cover photograph of military personnel marching with flags in The National Veterans Day Parade, Wednesday, Nov. 11, 2009 in downtown Birmingham, Ala. reproduced with permission of AP Photo/The Birmingham News, Bernard Troncale. Back cover photograph reproduced with permission of U.S. Air Force photo/SrA Jason Epley.

Every effort has been made to contact copyright holders of any material reproduced in this book. Any omissions will be rectified in subsequent printings if notice is given to the publisher.

Contents

What Is a Holiday?

A holiday is a special day.
People celebrate holidays.

4

Veterans Day is a holiday.
Veterans Day is in November.

Who Are Veterans?

The United States of America has a military.

The military guards the country.

There are five parts of the United States military.

The Navy, Coast Guard, Marine Corps, Air Force, and Army are the five parts of the military.

Veterans are people who have been part of the military.

Some veterans fought in wars.

Some veterans helped people in the United States.

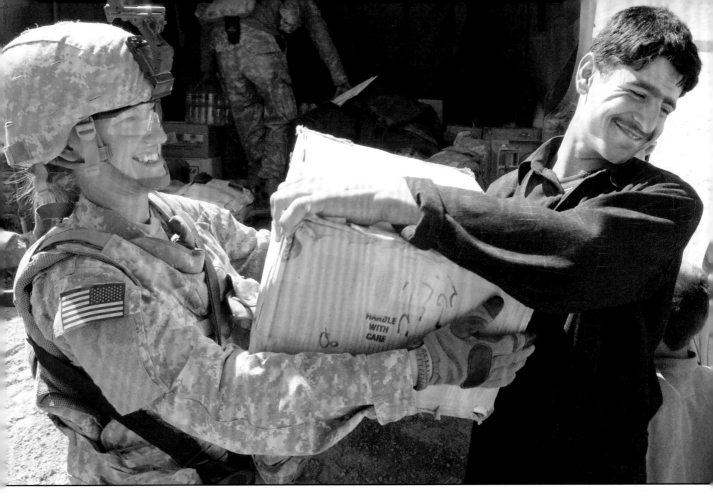

Some veterans helped people in different countries.

Celebrating Veterans Day

On Veterans Day people honor
veterans who fought in wars.

People honor veterans who served the
United States in times of peace.

15

On Veterans Day people say "thank you" to veterans for serving the country.

People remember veterans who
have died.

On Veterans Day the president of the United States visits the Tomb of the Unknown Soldier.

The president lays a wreath on the Tomb. This honors veterans everywhere.

Veterans Day Symbols

People fly the American flag on Veterans Day.

The flag reminds Americans to be thankful for the people who serve the country.

Calendar

Veterans Day is on November 11.

Picture Glossary

military the groups of people that protect a country. Together these groups are called the military.

soldier person who serves in the military

tomb place for remembering people who have died

Index

Note to Parents and Teachers

Before reading

Explain that on November 11, Americans celebrate Veterans Day, a holiday to honor people who have served in the military. Briefly explain what the armed forces are including the five branches. Ask the children for their impressions of the military and veterans – many will have family and/or friends who have served.

After reading

Create an opportunity to connect with veterans. Ask a local veteran to come in and talk to the children, arrange a visit to a local veteran's organization or have the children write letters to veterans asking them questions about their experiences in the military.